100 W

Elizabeth F
Midlands
Aberystwyth University, then in 1983 became a trainee journalist with the *Birmingham Post and Mail*. She has continued to work in journalism, mainly in a freelance capacity. At first, she specialized in writing about sport, but since 1990 has turned her hand to other subjects, including eating disorders, travel, women's issues and contemporary Christianity.

Other titles by Elizabeth Filleul in the same series available from Marshall Pickering

100 WAYS TO BE AT PEACE
100 WAYS TO INCREASE YOUR FAITH
100 WAYS TO PRAY MORE EFFECTIVELY

100 Ways
TO SHARE THE GOOD NEWS

Elizabeth Filleul

Marshall Pickering
An Imprint of HarperCollinsPublishers

Marshall Pickering is an Imprint of
HarperCollins*Religious*
Part of HarperCollins*Publishers*
77–85 Fulham Palace Road, London W6 8JB

First published in Great Britain
in 1995 by Marshall Pickering

1   3   5   7   9   10   8   6   4   2

Copyright in this compilation © 1995 Elizabeth Filleul

Elizabeth Filleul asserts the moral right to be
identified as the compiler of this work

A catalogue record for this book is
available from the British Library

ISBN 0 557 02967-6

Printed and bound in Great Britain by
Woolnough Bookbinding Limited,
Irthlingborough, Northamptonshire

CONDITIONS OF SALE
This book is sold subject to the condition that it
shall not, by way of trade or otherwise, be lent, re-sold,
hired out or otherwise circulated without the publisher's
prior consent in any form of binding or cover other
than that in which it is published and without a
similar condition including this condition being
imposed on the subsequent purchaser.

All rights reserved. No part of this publication may be
reproduced, stored in a retrieval system, or transmitted,
in any form or by any means, electronic, mechanical,
photocopying, recording or otherwise, without the prior
permission of the publishers.

Introduction

'A writer expresses himself in words that have been used before because they give his meaning better than he can give it himself, or because they are beautiful or witty, or because he expects them to touch a chord of association in his reader, or because he wishes to show that he is learned and well-read.' So claimed Francis George Fowler, adding that the last reason was the least worthy! But today's vogue for anthologies of quotations proves how right his comment was – words of wisdom, wit and beauty can strike a chord with readers irrespective of time or place.

100 Ways to Share the Good News is a book of quotations with a difference. It is intended for the Christian wishing to take seriously Christ's commission to go into all the world and make disciples. It is for the Christian who wants to spread the Gospel at a personal level, as well as through activities in their local church.

Spiritual teachers and evangelists down the ages have agreed that sharing the Good News involves more than standing up at a church mission and telling everybody your testimony. Here are some examples of what sharing the Good News might also entail:

- Sharing the Good News is being aware of God's

presence in everything around you – and pointing it out to your friends.

- Sharing the Good News is using whatever talents you have – whether in business, as a housekeeper, as an artist, as a flower-arranger – wisely, and in a way which brings honour to God.

- Sharing the Good News is being aware of injustices in the world, in the workplace, in your church – and speaking out against them because God is the God of justice.

- Sharing the Good News involves looking for good in people who are generally regarded as bad – and making those people aware that you recognize and appreciate their good points.

- Sharing the Good News means being a person of your word, who always thinks before making a promise, to be sure that it will be kept.

- Sharing the Good News involves being kind to other people, including total strangers, without expecting anything in return.

- Sharing the Good News means making prospective converts aware of the persecution that can accompany commitment, rather than only stressing the positive side of Christianity.

- Sharing the Good News involves obeying all of Christ's commandments, including asking God's blessing on those who dislike you.

- Sharing the Good News begins at home – by living out the Christian life among your family.

- Sharing the Good News is being as diligent about the small, 'unimportant' things in life as you are about the major things.

Sharing the Good News, then, involves *living* in the way Christ wants you to live. It is being the Good News, doing the Good News and telling of the Good News.

Down the centuries evangelists, spiritual writers, teachers and leaders have pin-pointed tried-and-tested ways of sharing the Good News. Many of their suggestions appear in this book. I urge you to go on to read their work, and unearth even more strategies to share the Gospel with your friends.

Additionally, I have included some quotations from secular sources. This is because secular people are the ones Christians are trying to reach – and sometimes God uses their words and ideas to show us how to communicate effectively with them.

The selected quotations show tremendous variety in strategies for introducing others to God. I have my personal favourites; you will too. What will become clear is that there is no one suggestion which will convert every single person at any one time. The ideas you choose will depend very much on your individual personality and – above all – on the personalities of your non-Christian friends.

Each quotation is accompanied by a suggestion for appropriate reflection or practical action. Some suggestions take the form of a question, inviting you to scrutinize aspects of your daily life. What does your lifestyle say to others about the God you worship?

This book is not a 'step-by-step' guide to being the world's best evangelist. Being a Christian and spreading the Gospel is not about Brownie points. But, by following the advice, you will find yourself thinking more deeply about the way in which you present the Good News to non-Christians: whether verbally or by the way you live.

See God in everything

All you big things bless the Lord
Mount Kilimanjaro and Lake Victoria
The Rift Valley and the Serengeti Plain
Fat baobabs and shady mango trees
All eucalyptus and tamarind trees
Bless the Lord
Praise and extol him for ever and ever.

All you tiny things bless the Lord
Busy black ants and hopping fleas
Wriggling tadpoles and mosquito larvae
Flying locusts and water drops
Pollen dust and tsetse flies
Millet seeds and dried dagga
Bless the Lord
Praise and extol him for ever and ever.

AFRICAN CANTICLE

🌿 See God in everything around you – and point him out to others.

Give someone a Bible

OUR Father, we thank you for the Bible which tells us the Christmas story. Thank you, too, for the writings, centuries before, which tell of the coming Saviour and King. Thank you for those who toiled and gave their lives so that we could have the Bible in our own language. Help us to understand your word . . . .
PRAYERS BEFORE WORSHIP

🙵 Give someone a Bible, or St John's gospel, so they can read about Jesus' earthly ministry for themselves. Follow this up with discussions about particular passages from time to time.

Consider non-discipleship

NON-discipleship costs abiding peace, a life penetrated throughout by love, faith that sees everything in the light of God's overriding governance for good, hopefulness that stands firm in the most discouraging of circumstances, power to do what is right and withstand the forces of evil. In short, it costs exactly that abundance of life Jesus said he came to bring.

DALLAS WILLARD, *The Spirit of the Disciplines*

> 🐝 Talk to a non-Christian about what they are missing out on in rejecting Christ.

Look out for loners

MY fiftieth year had come and gone,
I sat, a solitary man
In a crowded London shop,
An open book and empty cup
On the marble table-top.

While on the shop and street I gazed
My body of a sudden blazed;
And twenty minutes more or less
It seemed, so great my happiness,
That I was bless'd and I could bless.
W. B. YEATS, *Vacillation*

🐝 Go into a coffee shop and sit next to and talk to someone sitting on their own. Take a genuine interest in them and don't try to 'accomplish' anything by your action.

Offer to pray

NOBODY lives in this world without being laden with burdens, though each person's weight differs from another's. But Jesus said, 'Come unto me, all ye that labour and are heavy-laden, and I will give you rest.' How can we come to Jesus? Through prayer. When we lay down our burdens before Jesus, the Holy Spirit, who is sent by Jesus, will solve them.

PAUL YONGGI CHO, *Praying with Jesus*

🍂 Ask a troubled person you know if you can pray for them – either with them, or later on your own. But let them know you're praying.

Correct misconceptions

LORD, as you dispelled
the fears of a maiden mother
by whispering the promise of your presence,
so banish the world's misconceptions
about you and your ways.
FURTHER EVERYDAY PRAYERS

🌢 Correct a misconception a friend or colleague has about God and Christianity. Do it with kindness and gentleness – not as a rebuke.

Share your possessions

LORD, teach us to value our possessions in the right way. Help us never to think more of them than of people. Make us ready to use them freely for the good of others and to share them generously without grudging. Thank you for the beautiful things that we enjoy possessing. May our enjoyment be wholesome and right and may we hold lightly to all we own.

MARY BATCHELOR, *The Lion Prayer Collection*

🌿 Offer a friend the use of any material possession you have which they don't possess. Also, pray this prayer any time you feel yourself sliding into a more materialistic mind-set.

Be aware of your failings

WHY do you see the speck in your neighbour's eye, but do not notice the log in your own eye? Or how can you say to your neighbour, 'Friend, let me take out the speck in your eye,' when you yourself do not see the log in your own eye? You hypocrite, first take the log out of your own eye, and then you will see clearly to take the speck out of your neighbour's eye.

LUKE 6:41–2

🙋 Think of times when you have criticized someone else's faults while remaining oblivious of your own. Pray that you will be more aware of your own failings, and that you will think before you criticize.

Don't forget good people

IN listening to some presentations of the Gospel you get the impression that a man has to be a blackguard before Jesus Christ can do anything for him. It is true that Jesus Christ can make a saint out of any material, but the man down-and-out in sin is not the only crisis he deals with.

OSWALD CHAMBERS, *Conformed to His Image*

🕮 How would you introduce Jesus Christ to a person who leads a good, moral life, and is happy and content? Which of Jesus' commands do you think would most intrigue them?

Don't mention church!

Isn't it strange that people place so much emphasis upon going to church when there is not one command from Jesus to do so, and yet neglect the basic duties of our ordinary life which are commanded in every page of the gospels.

WILLIAM LAW,
A Serious Call to a Devout and Holy Life

🌿 The next time you talk to someone about the Lord, don't mention going to church. Talk instead about some of the things Jesus stressed – e.g. care of the poor and sick.

Introduce the Lord

LORD, today you made us known to friends we did not know,
And you have given us seats in homes which are not our own.
You have brought the distant near
And made a brother of a stranger,
Forgive us Lord . . .
We did not introduce you.

POLYNESIAN PRAYER

> Does everyone who knows you realize you know God? How are you going to introduce him to those who don't?

Don't make life harder for others

FORGIVE us if we have made work harder for others, by being careless, thoughtless, selfish and inconsiderate.

Forgive us if we have made faith harder for others, by laughing at things they hold precious, or casting doubts on things they hold dear.

Forgive us if we have made goodness harder for others, by setting them an example which would make it easier for them to go wrong.

Forgive us if we have made joy harder for others, by bringing gloom and depression through our grumbling discontent.

WILLIAM BARCLAY, *The Plain Man's Book of Prayers*

🙶 If, today, you feel you've made work, faith, goodness or joy harder for another person, phone or write to them now, asking their forgiveness.

Use your talents wisely

WE can't take any credit for our talents. It's how we use them that counts.
> MADELEINE L'ENGLE, *A Wrinkle in Time*

🐚 Are you using your talents wisely? Do they bring glory to God? Ask God to show you how you might use them best.

Are you patient and kind?

If I speak in the tongues of mortals and of angels, but do not have love, I am a noisy gong or a clanging cymbal. And if I have prophetic powers, and understand all mysteries and all knowledge, and if I have all faith, so as to remove mountains, but do not have love, I am nothing. If I give away my possessions, and if I hand over my body so that I may boast, but do not have love, I gain nothing.

Love is patient; love is kind; love is not envious or boastful or arrogant or rude. It does not insist on its own way; it is not irritable or resentful; it does not rejoice in wrongdoing, but rejoices in the truth. It bears all things, believes all things, hopes all things, endures all things.

Love never ends.

1 CORINTHIANS 13:1–8

🔖 Replace the word 'love' in the second paragraph with your own name. Are you patient and kind, not envious or boastful? Ask God to help you to attain Paul's definition of love.

Provide a venue for non-Christians

THE Church exists for the sake of those outside it.
WILLIAM TEMPLE

🐾 How might your church be used by non-churchgoers? Think of some activities – e.g. a mum's and tots group, charity meeting place, keep-fit class, youth club – which could possibly be held there. Discuss them with your church leadership. If your church already provides services for the community, see if you can get involved in them.

Leave a legacy of love

L ET us live in such a way
That when we die
Our love will survive
And continue to grow.
Amen.
MICHAEL LEUNIG, *Common Prayer Collection*

🙠 When you die, how do you want people to remember you? Are there any negative habits or qualities you would not want people to remember? If so, try to eradicate them from your life.

Be kind

No act of kindness, no matter how small, is ever wasted.

AESOP, *The Lion and the Mouse*

🐾 Today, go out of your way to be kind to everybody you meet.

Be an instrument of peace

Lord, make me an instrument of your peace. Where there is hatred, let me sow love; where there is injury, pardon; where there is doubt, faith; where there is despair, hope; where there is darkness, light; and where there is sadness, joy.

O divine Master, grant that I may not so much seek to be consoled as to console; to be understood as to understand; to be loved as to love. For it is in giving that we receive; it is in pardoning that we are pardoned; and it is in dying that we are born to eternal life.

St Francis of Assisi

🙞 Write that prayer in your diary or Bible and make it your own.

Record your testimony

ONE generation shall laud your works to another,
   and shall declare your mighty acts.
On the glorious splendour of your majesty,
   and on your wondrous works, I will meditate.
The might of your awesome deeds shall be proclaimed,
   and I will declare you greatness.
They shall celebrate the fame of your abundant goodness,
   and shall sing aloud of your righteousness.

PSALM 145:4–7

🌢 Write down your testimony, or record it on cassette
or video, ensuring the focus is on God, not yourself,
and put it away for future generations to find.

Talk about persecution

MANY Christians think Christianity is intrinsically attractive. They believe that their friends would soon be converted if they experienced real worship, saw an authentic miracle, heard an outstanding sermon or met a Christ-like person. They're sure that more people would flock to the faith if more believers went to 'signs and wonders' conferences, attended evangelism courses, and structured their churches on a New Testament pattern. They miss the truth of the eighth Beatitude.

Authentic Christianity has always been deeply repugnant to ordinary people. The real followers of Jesus will always be persecuted, because there is something about Jesus which is deeply disturbing. He's different. And humanity won't accept people who are different.

TIM PAIN

🙢 In which ways have you been persecuted for your faith? Talk about it – and how you deal with it – with someone who is thinking of becoming a Christian.

Oppose injustice

INJUSTICE anywhere is a threat to justice everywhere.

MARTIN LUTHER KING

❧ The next time you see an injustice (in the world, at work, in your church), speak out against it. Let everyone know you do not approve of what is going on.

Drop non-Christian habits

IN Africa, a Christian teacher used to go off on weekends and drink. He became drunk and went into a native hut and slept. When he woke up, an old man was seated looking at him. The old man asked him who he was, and was told that he was a Christian. When he asked the old man who he was, he replied: 'I'm not a Christian, but if I were, I wouldn't be living the way you are – I'd really live as a Christian.' This awakened the teacher; he was really converted and lived a Christian life afterward – converted by an unconverted man!

E. STANLEY JONES, *Conversion*

🕿 Is there a habit in your life that might lead others to think you are not a Christian? If so, resolve to break it.

Eat simply

FATHER of all the peoples,
We who can eat our fill
Ask as your gift at harvest
A dedicated will.

Show us our hungry brothers,
Teach us that we must care,
Help us to live more simply
Because we want to share.

For you, who fed the hungry,
May we so break our bread
In constant, costly giving
That others may be fed.

LILIAN COX

🌣 Spend one day eating cheap, simple meals – then donate the money you would usually have spent on your food to charity.

Be 'cruel' to be kind

FOR even though I made you sorry with my letter, I do not regret it (though I did regret it, for I see that I grieved you with that letter, though only briefly). Now I rejoice, not because you were grieved, but because your grief led to repentance; for you felt a godly grief, so that you were not harmed in any way by us. For godly grief produces a repentance that leads to salvation and brings no regret, but worldly grief produces death.

2 CORINTHIANS 7:8–10

🙢 Don't shrink from rebuking a person, if you feel it will draw them closer to God. However, do it sensitively and with kindness.

Talk about the Lord

PAY attention to the conversation of the average practising Christian. You might spend from the first of January to the end of December and never hear them speak about their faith. They scarcely even mention the name of Jesus Christ at all. On Sunday afternoon, what will they talk about at the dinner table? It will not be about the minister's sermon, unless they want to point out some faults.

Do they ever talk about what Jesus said and did? What he suffered for us? When we go to each other's houses, what will we talk about? I have concluded this: you will not know how to get to heaven simply by eavesdropping on the conversations of the members of the Church! We talk too little about our Lord.

CHARLES SPURGEON,
Spiritual Revival, the Want of the Church

🌿 Talk openly about your faith to a non-believer at some point today.

Treat others as God treats you

When God was merciful to us, we learned to be merciful with our brethren. When we received forgiveness instead of judgement, we, too, were ready to forgive our brethren. What God did to us, we then owed to others. The more we received, the more we were able to give; and the more meagre our brotherly love, the less were we living by God's mercy and love.
DIETRICH BONHOEFFER, *Life Together*

🌱 This week, when God forgives you for something you've done or not done, remember to forgive other people for things *they* have done or failed to do.

Look for good where you don't expect it

GIVE me the ability to see good things
in unexpected places and talents in unexpected people,
And give me, O Lord, the grace to tell them so.

ANONYMOUS

> Today, look for and praise a good point or talent in a person generally regarded as difficult or dull.

Brighten your home!

FEW are born to do the great work of the world, but the work that all can do is to make a small home circle brighter and better.
GEORGE ELIOT

🌢 Think of something you can do to make your home a 'brighter and better' place for all your family. Do it with love.

Be a Good Samaritan

A man was going down from Jerusalem to Jericho, and fell into the hands of robbers, who stripped him, beat him, and went away, leaving him half dead. Now by chance a priest was going down that road; and when he saw him, he passed by on the other side. So likewise a Levite, when he came to the place and saw him, passed by on the other side. But a Samaritan while travelling came near him; and when he saw him, he was moved with pity. He went to him and bandaged his wounds, having poured oil and wine on them. Then he put him on his own animal, brought him to an inn, and took care of him. The next day he took out two denarii, gave them to the innkeeper, and said, 'Take care of him; and when I come back, I will repay you whatever more you spend.' Which of these three, do you think, was a neighbour to the man who fell into the hands of the robbers?

LUKE 10:30-7

🌿 Do you know of someone who is being persecuted for their non-Christian religious beliefs? How can you express your concern for their welfare? If you know of no one personally, perhaps there is a persecuted group in Britain or elsewhere in the world to whom you could donate money, food or clothing.

Be zealous

SINS of omission are avoiding to do good of any kind when we have the opportunity. We must beware of these sins and, instead, be zealous of good works. Do all the good you possibly can to the bodies and souls of your neighbours. Be active. Give no place to laziness. Be always busy, losing no shred of time. Whatever your hand finds to do, do it with all your might.
JOHN WESLEY, *Christian Perfection*

🌿 Today, try to fill every moment of your time. Whenever the opportunity to do good of any kind comes along, take it.

Be silent

AND just so
the suffering servant, Isaiah,
did not open his mouth,
and Jesus, before his accusers,
was silent.

Goodness does not argue,
it speaks for itself.

FRANK TOPPING, *Wings of the Morning*

🍃 Think of those times when you spoke out when it would have been better to say nothing. When a similar situation occurs, remember to be silent.

Never be disheartened

SOMETIMES when I thought I had done the least, then it developed that the most had been accomplished; and at other times when I thought I had really gotten hold of them, I found that I had fished for nothing.

JOHN BUNYAN,
Grace Abounding to the Chief of Sinners

🙢 Never be disheartened when your attempts to share the Gospel seem to fall on deaf ears. Remember, you may have sown a seed that will take root in the future.

Talk about what you know

IF a bridge is to be built, the Church may remind the engineer that it is his obligation to provide a safe bridge, but it is not entitled to tell him how to build it or whether his design meets this requirement.

WILLIAM TEMPLE, *Christianity and Social Order*

🍃 What is your area of expertise? How does it relate to your faith? How can you bring a Christian influence to your skills?

Be available

FAITH, like light, should always be simple and unbending; while love, like warmth, should beam forth on every side, and bend to every necessity of our brethren.

MARTIN LUTHER

🌿 Show your love to everyone around you by always being available to help or listen.

Pray about the sufferings of those you dislike

If we could read the secret history of our enemies, we should find in each man's life sorrow and suffering enough to disarm all hostility.

HENRY WADSWORTH LONGFELLOW

🐾 Think of someone you don't like at work, in your community or even at church. What do you really know about their lives? Like everyone else they will have their troubles and sufferings. Try to befriend them and pray about any problems you discover they have.

Join forces

AFTER this the Lord appointed seventy others and sent them on ahead of him in pairs to every town and place where he himself intended to go. He said to them, 'The harvest is plentiful, but the labourers are few; therefore ask the Lord of the harvest to send out labourers into his harvest.'
LUKE 10:1–2

🌿 Join forces with another Christian in your church and work out a plan for personal evangelism in your community.

Talk to the pressurized

I think . . . when a person is under a lot of pressure they start to question the whys and wherefores of life. That's why people at university become Christians – they start asking questions about the meaning of life. It's the same in sport, where you lay yourself completely on the line. You realize there must be something more to life.

NICKY SLATER

🍃 Think of someone you know who is under pressure and beginning to question the meaning of life. Invite them to your home for coffee and a chat.

Let Christ use you

CHRIST has no body now on earth but yours.
Yours are the only hands with which he can do his work,
Yours are the only feet through which he can go about the world,
Yours are the only eyes through which his compassion can shine forth upon a troubled world.
Christ has no body now on earth but yours.

ST TERESA OF AVILA

🌿 How does Christ want to work through you to show his compassion in the world today? Tell him that you are willing to go wherever and do whatever he wants.

Hug somebody!

GIVE me a HUG
'I care' without words
When I'm suffering
I don't need words
I just need to know you are there
That someone would notice if I disappeared
And if I matter to you
And I matter to God
then life is worth living.

RAE WILLIAMS, *A Tapestry of Voices*

🌿 Give someone a hug to show them that you care.

Reach out to 'misfits'

WHEN I pick up a person from the streets hungry, I give him a plate of rice, a piece of bread, and I have satisfied that hunger; but a person that is shut out, that feels unwanted, unloved, terrified, the person that has been thrown out of society – how much more difficult it is to remove that hunger.

MOTHER TERESA

❧ Think of a way you can reach out to someone who seems a 'misfit' in society – and act upon it.

Give to those who ask

So I say to you, Ask, and it will be given you; search, and you will find; knock, and the door will be opened for you. For everyone who asks receives, and everyone who searches finds, and for everyone who knocks the door will be opened.

LUKE 11:9–10

> 🌺 Make Jesus' actions to us here, yours to other people.

Send flowers

What brings joy to the heart is not so much the friend's gift as the friend's love.
St Aelred of Rievaulx

🌺 Send flowers to a treasured friend to show how much you love and value them.

Don't be denominational

THE first goal he [Jesus] set forth for the early Church was to use his all-encompassing power and authority to make disciples.... Having made disciples, these alone were to be baptized into the name of the Father, and of the Son, and of the Holy Spirit. With this twofold preparation they were to be taught to treasure and keep 'all things whatsoever I have commanded you'. The Christian Church of the first century resulted from following this plan for church growth....

But in place of Christ's plan, historical drift has substituted: 'Make converts (to a particular faith and practice) and baptize them into church membership.'

DALLAS WILLARD, *The Spirit of the Disciplines*

🌿 Stop encouraging your non-Christian friends to come along to your church, and encourage them to read the gospels instead.

Be hospitable

L ORD, I'm so glad
We don't have to be creative geniuses
Or serve elegant gourmet meals
To make our guests feel warm and wanted.
We need rather to expose them to love
And introduce them to laughter.
We need to listen and never drown them out.
Above all, we need to remember
That there is no substitute –
None whatever –
For genuine caring.
RUTH HARMS CALKIN

❧ Invite someone to your home for a coffee or a simple meal, and genuinely enjoy their company.

Campaign for the oppressed

MANY slaves on the continent are oppressed, and their cries have reached the ears of the Most High! Such is the purity and certainty of his judgements that he cannot be partial in our favour. In infinite love and goodness he has opened our understandings from one time to another concerning our duty toward this people, and it is not a time for delay.

JOHN WOOLMAN, *Journal*

🕭 Many people are oppressed today because of their race, sex or religious or political views. Pray for their freedom – and join a group which campaigns on their behalf.

Be a Christian family

EACH of you, however, should love his wife as himself, and a wife should respect her husband. Children, obey your parents in the Lord, for this is right. 'Honour your father and mother' – this is the first commandment with a promise: 'so that it may be well with you and you may live long on the earth.' And, fathers, do not provoke your children to anger, but bring them up in the discipline and instruction of the Lord.
EPHESIANS 5:33–6:4

🙰 What does the behaviour of your family, at home and outside, say about your devotion to Christ? Does this behaviour need changing in any way? Call a family meeting to discuss the matter.

Encourage searching

ACCEPTING one religion without exploring others isn't sensible. That's why so many young people in particular stop believing in God – because they didn't actively search for him, they were just indoctrinated.

NON-CHRISTIAN STUDENT

🐾 Rather than telling of what God has done for you, encourage a sceptic to begin to search for God. Suggest some useful material which might start them on their way.

Don't base others' experiences on your own

THE things that happen to me are not the things that will happen to the next man, and I have no right to try to crush him into the little box of my own experience. It is so easy to be wrong, so easy to decide that because God did 'X' on Tuesday, he will do 'X' on Wednesday; so easy to preach our own salvation as the way things should be, instead of acknowledging the excitingly complex and creative nature of God's dealings with men.

ADRIAN PLASS,
The Growing Up Pains of Adrian Plass

🌿 Don't assume that what God does in your life, he will do in someone else's. Listen to other people's experiences, without jumping in with your view of what God will do.

Never criticize what you don't understand

O Lord, help me not to despise or oppose what I do not understand.

WILLIAM PENN

🌿 Resolve never to be critical or any belief or theory that you know nothing about. Instead, read about it and ask other people about it. Try to find common ground as a starting-point for a discussion on Christianity.

Keep your promises

And now, dear friends, in all your words, in all your business and employments, have a care of breaking your words and promises to any people. Consider beforehand, that you may be able to perform and fulfil both your words and promises to people, that your yea be yea and nay, nay in all things, which Christ has set up instead of an oath.

Therefore, all are to consider aforehand, before they speak their yea, yea, what they are able to perform. It will preserve you out of all rash, hasty words and promises, for such kind of inconsiderate and rash speaking is not in the everlasting covenant of light, life and grace.

George Fox, *Letters*

❧ From this moment, only ever make promises that you know you can keep.

Be clear

Tongues then are a sign not for believers but for unbelievers, while prophecy is not for unbelievers but for believers. If, therefore, the whole church comes together and all speak in tongues, and outsiders or unbelievers enter, will they not say that you are out of your mind? But if all prophesy, an unbeliever or outsider who enters is reproved by all and called to account by all. After the secrets of the unbeliever's heart are disclosed, that person will bow down before God and worship him, declaring, 'God is really among you.'

1 Corinthians 14:22–5

🌠 Do you ever leave non-believers puzzled or confused – perhaps by speaking in Christian jargon which they do not understand? Work out ways in which you can talk plainly to non-Christians about your faith.

Smile at a stranger

A smile costs nothing, but gives much. It enriches those who receive without making poorer those who give; it takes but a moment, but the memory of it lasts forever.

ANONYMOUS

🍃 Smile at the first person you meet on the way to work or the shops today. Notice their reaction, and then try to keep up the habit throughout the day.

Complete outstanding tasks

HERE is the unformed side of life's relationships – the letters to be written, the friends to be visited, the journey to be undertaken, the suffering to be met by food, or nursing, care or fellowship. Here is the social wrong to be resisted, the piece of interpretive work to be undertaken, the command to 'rebuild my churches', the article to be written, the wrong to be forgiven, the grudge to be dropped, the relationship to be set right, the willingness to serve God in the interior court by clear honest thinking, and the refusal to turn out shoddy work.

DOUGLAS V. STEERE, *Prayer and Worship*

🍂 What outstanding tasks have you been putting off? Remember, the things you *don't* do can say as much about you as the things you *do* do. Make a list of them and resolve to complete at least one every day this week until they are finished.

Take nobody for granted

WHEN we examine our deepest resentments we find that invariably, at their roots, lies the fact that someone has not respected us. How have they not respected us? Usually the violation, on the surface, is not blatant. Almost always it is subtle: they have taken us for granted; they have assumed that they have understood us and our motives, boxed us in with their own preconceived notions; not respected our uniqueness, mystery and complexity; and taken as owed to them what we can only offer as gift. That is the illusion of familiarity and it is that which is expressed in the axiom: *familiarity breeds contempt.*

RONALD ROLHEISER, *The Shattered Lantern*

🙢 Determine never to take another person for granted, but to appreciate their uniqueness and complexity. After a week, examine how well you achieved this resolve.

Remember God loves everybody

AND because of his great and everlasting love, God makes no distinction in the love he has for the blessed soul of Christ, and that which he has for the lowliest soul to be saved.

ST JULIAN OF NORWICH

> Whoever you meet today, remember that God loves them as much as he loved his own Son, and wants to welcome them into his kingdom. Tell the person of God's great love for them.

Befriend a prisoner

PEOPLE cannot remain good unless good is expected of them.
BERTOLD BRECHT

🌸 Write to or visit a prisoner on a regular basis. Pray for them to come to know Christ.

Care for the lonely

FATHER, we pray for all lonely people, especially those who coming home to an empty house stand at the door hesitant and afraid to enter. May all who stand on any doorway with fear in their hearts, like the two on the Emmaus road, ask the living one in. Then, by his grace, may they find that in loneliness they are never alone and that he peoples empty rooms with his presence.

E. M. FARR

🙢 Visit someone who lives on their own. Take a box of chocolates, a bottle of wine or some other gift and spend a few hours with them.

Treat a child

AND he who gives a child a treat
Makes joy-bells sing in heaven's street,
And he who gives a child a home
Builds palaces in Kingdom come,
And she who gives a baby birth
Brings Saviour Christ again to earth.
JOHN MASEFIELD, *The Everlasting Mercy*

🌿 Buy a treat for a child and give it to someone in the children's ward at your local hospital, or to a child who you know is in real need.

Influence the media

PERHAPS we ought to be writing to the programme-makers, not only with the usual complaints about sex and violence, but to point out (politely) examples of over-simplification or inaccuracy in portrayals of Christian characters. Just as important, the shapers and makers need to be praised when they have clearly made an effort to get it right.

NAOMI STARKEY

🌿 Look out for inaccurate portrayals of Christians on TV. Write to the programme-makers with positive suggestions for future portrayals or new programme ideas.

Forgive people's weaknesses

THE truly humble person will not only look admirably at the strengths of others, but will also look with great forgiveness upon the weaknesses of others. The truly humble person will try to see how the sinful deeds done by others were committed because the person was unenlightened or misled, concluding that if the person had the same benefits and helps that he had, they would not have committed any such evil, but rather, would have done much good.

JEREMY TAYLOR,
The Rule and Exercises of Holy Living

€ Today, when someone does something you consider foolish, forgive them, reminding yourself, 'There, but for the grace of God, go I.'

Care for your body

Do you not know that your bodies are members of Christ? . . . Or do you not know that your body is a temple of the Holy Spirit within you, which you have from God, and that you are not your own? For you were bought with a price: therefore glorify God in your body.

1 CORINTHIANS 6:15A, 19–20

🙦 Resolve to eat more healthily, take more exercise or go to bed earlier to ensure your body has the care it needs.

Think of yourself

We wish to see others severely reprimanded; yet we are unwilling to be corrected ourselves. We wish to restrict the liberty of others, but are not willing to be denied anything ourselves. We wish others to be bound by rules, yet we will not let ourselves be bound. It is amply evident, therefore, that we seldom consider our neighbour in the same light as ourselves. Yet, if all men were perfect, what should we have to bear with in others for Christ's sake?

THOMAS À KEMPIS, *The Imitation of Christ*

🌿 Try never to approve a ruling – whether in the country, at church, at work or at home – if you would not like it applied to yourself.

Feed the needy

When you give a luncheon or a dinner, do not invite your friends or your brothers or your relatives or rich neighbours, in case they may invite you in return, and you would be repaid. But when you give a banquet, invite the poor, the crippled, the lame and the blind. And you will be blessed, because they cannot repay you, for you will be repaid at the resurrection of the righteous.

Luke 14:12–14

🍃 Invite for a meal someone who you know is unable, because of circumstances, to invite you back. Be careful not to treat them as 'Lord or Lady Bountiful', but with genuine interest.

Don't complain about the weather

THANK you for the sunshine bright,
Thank you for the morning light.
Thank you for the rain and showers.
Thank you for the fruit and flowers.
Thank you for each tall green tree.
Thank you for the sand and sea.
Thank you for the winds that blow.
Thank you for the frost and snow.
H. WIDDOWS

🌿 Don't join in complaints about the weather. Accept that whatever the weather, it is good for somebody. Also, marvel at the forces at work and the changes brought about by weather of all kinds.

Pray that others see Jesus in you

So grant that through this day all with whom we work, and all whom we meet, may see in us the reflection of the Master, whose we are, and whom we seek to serve.

WILLIAM BARCLAY

🙏 Ask God that all who you meet today will see the love of Jesus reflected in you.

Accept one another

FATHER, bless the family of the Church. May we accept one another as brothers and sisters, finding strength and joy in our life together. May we be a family open to all the families of mankind that, in the Church, they may overcome all the hostilities and prejudices that might otherwise drive them apart.
MORE EVERYDAY PRAYERS

🕯 Make friends with any other Christians you meet, whatever their denomination. Show non-believers that Christians can be unified.

Pray for politicians

O God, King of kings and Lord of lords,
We pray today for statesmen, leaders and rulers.
May they be quiet in spirit, clear in judgement,
   able to understand the issues that face them.
May they think often of the common people on whose
   behalf they must speak and act.
May they remember that in keeping your laws is man's
   only good and happiness.
Grant them patience, grant them courage,
   grant them foresight and great faith.
In their anxieties be their security,
   in their opportunities be their inspiration.
By their plans and their actions may your kingdom
   come, your will be done.

LILIAN COX

> Write to your local MP about a matter which bothers you as a Christian. Pray for your local MP, that he will look to God for guidance in decisions he must make.

Do as you would be done by

Do to others as you would have them do to you.
LUKE 6:31

🌺 What would you most like someone to do for you now? Give you a hug? Phone you? Send you flowers? Straight away, do that very thing for someone else.

Tell them everything

CONVERSION is a gift and an achievement. It is the act of a moment and the work of a lifetime.

E. STANLEY JONES, *Conversion*

🕮 Explain to interested non-Christian friends that being converted is only the beginning of the Christian life – not a glorious end.

Talk to cult members

ALL the time I was knocking on doors as a Jehovah's Witness, no one ever told me about the fatherhood of God or his adoption of us. No one ever pointed out how I was being misled by the Watchtower Society. It's sad to think that there are over 127,000 JWs in Britain, who sincerely love God and want to obey him, yet have never heard of the wonderful blessings that can be theirs through Christ Jesus.

A FORMER JEHOVAH'S WITNESS

🌿 The next time you meet a member of a sect or cult, talk to them about the fatherhood of God.

Lift someone up to God

IT is because of this [God's] tender love for you that I need not ask anything of God for you. All I need to do is lift you before his face.

    CATHERINE OF GENOA, *Life and Teachings*

> Pray for a hurting person. Don't ask anything specific for them – just let God do what he knows is best.

Reach downward

WINDOWS open outward as well as upward. Windows open *especially* downward where people need the most!

FRANK LAUBACH, *Letters by a Modern Mystic*

🙞 Think of someone you can 'reach downward' to this week. What is that person's greatest need at the moment? How you can help to meet it?

Be happy!

WHOEVER is happy will make others happy too. He who has courage and faith will never perish in misery.
The Diary of Anne Frank

🌺 Show everybody how happy you are – smile, sing, laugh. If you aren't happy, explore the reasons why and take steps to remedy the situation – in the short and long term.

Make public your forgiveness

I bear no ill-will against those responsible for this. That sort of talk will not bring her back to life. I know that there has to be a plan even though we might not understand it. God is good and we shall meet again.
GORDON WILSON, *after the murder of his daughter Marie by an IRA bomb at the Enniskillen Rememberance Day Service, 8 November 1986.*

🌢 When you forgive someone for sinning against you, make sure everyone knows that you have forgiven – and why.

Give your all

WHATEVER your task, put yourselves into it, as done for the Lord and not for your masters, since you know that from the Lord you will receive the inheritance as your reward; you serve the Lord Christ.

COLOSSIANS 3:23–4

🌿 Give your all to your daily tasks, reminding yourself you are doing them for God.

Pray unceasingly

An unbeliever once mockingly begged Catherine of Siena that she pray for his soul. She prayed by day and by night, and the power of renovation disarmed and brought him to his knees. I know of a Japanese girl whose father had found a whole chain of reverses too much for him to meet normally and who had taken the alcoholic short cut. She prayed for him hour after hour until the time came when he yielded, gave up drink, committed his life to the centre of divine love he had experienced, and with the help and love of his devoted family he has continued a new way of life.

Douglas V. Steere, *Prayer and Worship*

🍂 Tell one of your non-believing friends that you intend to pray for them every day until they are converted – and do so.

Get your hands dirty

CHRISTIANS should be 'doing' Good News as well as speaking it. The Church needs to get its hands dirty, to start reaching out to people in loving action.

FRAN BECKETT

> Do some voluntary work for a charity – even if you can manage only an hour per week, it will make a difference to someone else's life.

Demonstrate God's importance

BE an example to all of denying yourself and taking up your cross daily. Let others see that you are not interested in any pleasure that does not bring you nearer to God.

JOHN WESLEY, *Christian Perfection*

🌿 For a while, drop any activities which draw you away from God rather than closer to him. Tell other people why you are giving up those activities. Think of how the time usually taken up by those activities can be used for God's glory.

Make a good impression

First impressions are the most lasting.

ANONYMOUS

🌿 The next occasion you meet someone for the first time, ask yourself what you would most like them to remember about you. Then act upon it.

Understand other religions

IN our dealings with one another, let us be more eager to understand those who differ from us than either to refute them or press upon them our own tradition.
WILLIAM TEMPLE

🔖 Read a book or watch a TV documentary on another religion. Try to understand why people practise that religion. Then try and talk to people of that religion sensitively about Christianity.

Befriend a homeless person

WE need to see the homeless for who they are and see that we need them as much as they need us. Only by recognizing that we're all roommates in the house of life together can we clear up our house and make it liveable again.

WILLIAM LAWYER

> Chat to the next homeless person you see. Try to befriend them. Get to know all about them. Learn from them and see how much they enrich your life.

Do good in secret

To succeed in being a secret doer of good is perhaps the highest aim a Christian can have. Read the gospels with an open mind, and you may be surprised to find out how often this is reiterated by the Son of God himself. He had some harsh things to say about the show-off Pharisees, and about those who regularly 'pass by on the other side'.
EILEEN MITSON

🙞 Help someone in need without telling anybody you have done so. Try to act in this way as often as you can.

Live quietly

BUT we urge you, beloved, to do so more and more, to aspire to live quietly, to mind your own affairs, and to work with your hands, as we directed you, so that you may behave properly toward outsiders and be dependent on no one.

1 THESSALONIANS 4:10-12

🌿 Lead a quiet life, being friendly with your neighbours but never interfering in their business. That said, take a real and genuine interest in them.

Lighten someone's burden

No one is useless in this world who lightens the burden of it to anyone else.
CHARLES DICKENS

🌺 Is there someone in your family, street, workplace or church who looks after an elderly or disabled relative full-time? Offer to go round and sit with the relative some time, so that the carer can arrange a day or evening out.

Be different

By living in a way which is indistinguishable from our neighbours, we show that we have bowed to the pressure of the advertisers' lies and have stopped believing the simple word of Jesus: 'Do not say "What are we to eat? What are we to drink? What are we to wear?" It is the pagans who set their hearts on these things.'

Our wardrobes, our possessions, our meal tables, our fridges, our vehicles, our bank balances, our homes, our holidays, all announce to the world what sort of God we serve, what matters most in our everyday lives, and how much we care about our siblings overseas.

TIM PAIN

> Sell one of your material possessions and give the money to a charity which helps the poor.

Care about the small things in life

FAITHFULNESS in little things is a big thing.
JOHN CHRYSOSTOM

🕮 Today, be diligent about what you consider the less important things in your life – they may be very important to someone else.

Be fair and honest

Do rightly, whether you be tradesmen, of what calling or profession or sort so ever, or husbandmen. Do rightly, justly, truly, holily, especially to all people in all things; and that is according to that of God in everyone, and the witness of God, and the wisdom of God, and the life of God in yourselves.

GEORGE FOX, *Letters*

> Be fair and honest with people at work or home. If there's someone you haven't been fair or honest towards recently, ask their forgiveness.

Forgive somebody

FORGIVE, like the Lord that you love – or become like the enemy you hate.
CARDINAL GORDON GRAY

۶ Tell someone who has wronged you recently that you forgive them.

Always encourage

CORRECTION does much, but encouragement does more. Encouragement after censure is as the sun after a shower.

JOHANN WOLFGANG VON GOETHE

> Make a point of always encouraging anybody you have to censure, whether at home, at work, or at church. Your encouragement should not come as an afterthought but as part of a full response.

Follow sport

WHEN church members are involved in secular [sports] clubs, it is essential that the church regards them as missionaries. The command of Jesus is to go into all the world and make disciples – and that includes the world of sport. . . . Sport is part of God's plan for his people and it brings pleasure to him as much as any other human activity.

CHRISTIANS IN SPORT

🙠 If you enjoy a sport, join a local club as a player or spectator. Pray for club members and talk to them about your faith.

Make the Gospel accessible

THE Gospel... has to be put to people in a way which is accessible to them and opens the doors of their imagination, instead of shutting them out by rules, regulations and cultural barriers.

PENELOPE WILCOCK

> Would non-Christian women, ethnic groups and homosexuals feel welcome at your church and sense that God was personally interested in their welfare? Think of ways of making more people welcome – perhaps get together with church friends to come up with some ideas.

Comfort others

COMFORT every sufferer
Watching late in pain;
Those who plan some evil
From their sin restrain.
S. BARING-GOULD, *Now the day is over*

🙋 Try never to miss the opportunity to comfort a troubled person or to try to prevent someone from sinning against God.

Expect nothing in return

THE best portion of a good man's life
His little, nameless, unremembered acts
Of kindness and of love.

WILLIAM WORDSWORTH

🌱 Today, do someone a kindness and expect nothing in return.

Speak of the sorrow

I like to think of God being joyous as well as a just God. But Christianity also has an answer for sorrow – it accepts that life for a great many people on earth is not joyous, good or happy, and we have this doctrine of God coming down and sharing the agonies as well as the joys of human life.
P. D. JAMES

🌱 Not everyone is happy. Talk about the way Jesus identifies with people's sorrow with someone you know is experiencing a bad patch.

Exploit any labels

I was delighted with [being given] the feminist label, partly because I was concerned about women, and partly because secular women's and university groups picked up on it and invited me to speak. This gave me an opportunity to talk to them about Christianity and Jesus' view of worth.

ELAINE STORKEY

🐾 Are you known for any views or beliefs other than for your Christianity? How can you use those beliefs to introduce people to Christ?

Give credit to God

I find that financial or career success can be very humbling, and I go on my knees and say to God's Spirit within me: 'Thank you, thank you for what you've given me. Help me never to take it for granted and misuse it and help me to give of you to other people.' If God's put me in the position of being able to communicate with other people, then I must not abuse that position and I must use it for him.

DAVID SUCHET

☙ Thank God for all the gifts he has given you and remember to give him public credit for it.

Examine your lifestyle

ONE must not always think so much about what one should do, but rather what one should be. Our works do not enable us, but we must enable our works.

MEISTER ECKHART

🕭 Cast a critical eye over your activities of the past week. Were you too busy doing Christian things to *be* a Christian?

Don't preach — be practical!

Go into the street and give one man a lecture on morality, and another a shilling, and see which will respect you most.
SAMUEL JOHNSON

🌿 Resolve never to preach Christianity in cases where it is better to practise it.

Be truthful

So then, putting away falsehood, let all of us speak the truth to our neighbours, for we are members of one another. Be angry but do not sin; do not let the sun go down on your anger, and do not make room for the devil.

EPHESIANS 4:25–7

> Ask God to show you when to tell the truth, and when it is best to keep the truth to yourself.

Learn from past mistakes

I F you don't learn from your mistakes, there's no point making them.
ANONYMOUS

🕿 Think about those times when your attempts to introduce someone to the Gospel failed or led to conflict – ask yourself where you went wrong. Ask God to help you not to repeat those mistakes with the next non-Christian you meet.

Acknowledgements

My thanks are due to the following people who either directly or indirectly helped me to compile this book: members of the Endowed Mission Hall in Rowley Regis who kindly lent me various spiritual classics; Bruce Clift and Jane Foulkes for introducing me to other useful books; my parents Vera and Richard Round and then-fiancé (now my husband), Grant Filleul who gave me space in which to work; and Christine Smith, editorial director of Marshall Pickering, for her help and encouragement, and for commissioning me in the first place.

The acknowledgement pages constitute an extension of the copyright pages.

Abingdon Press, for excerpts from the following:
1. *Conversion* by E. Stanley Jones.
2. *Life and Teachings* by Catherine of Genoa and *Rule and Exercises of Holy Living*, from *The Fellowship of the Saints* by Thomas S. Kepler, copyright 1947 by Stone & Peers, copyright renewal 1976 by Florence Tennant Kepler.
3. *Christian Perfection* by John Wesley.

Friends United Press, for excerpts from *Prayer and Worship*, by Douglas V. Steere.

HarperCollins, for excerpts from the following:
1. *The Plain Man's Book of Prayer* by William Barclay.
2. *Life Together* by Dietrich Bonhoeffer.
3. *Conformed to His Image* by Oswald Chambers.
4. *The Growing Up Pains of Adrian Plass* by Adrian Plass.
5. *The Spirit of the Disciplines* by Dallas Willard.

HarperCollins*Religious*, Melbourne, Australia, for excerpts from *Common Prayer Collection* by Michael Leunig.

Hodder and Stoughton, for excerpts from *The Shattered Lantern* by Ronald Rolheiser.

Lion Publishing, for prayers from *The Lion Prayer Collection* by Mary Batchelor.

Lutterworth Press, for excerpts from *Wings of the Morning* by Frank Topping.

Mowbray, for excerpts from *More Everyday Prayers: Further Everyday Prayers*.

Oxford University Press, for an excerpt from *The Journal and Major Essays of John Woolman*, edited by Phillips P. Moulton.

Thomas Nelson Inc., for excerpts from *The Imitation of Christ* by Thomas à Kempis, translated by E. M. Blaiklock.

New Reader's Press, for excerpts from *Letters by a Modern Mystic* by Frank Laubach.

Penguin Books, for excerpts from the following:
1. *Revelations of Divine Love*, by Julian of Norwich.
2. *Christianity and Social Order* by William Temple.

All Bible quotations are taken from the NRSV.

Every effort has been made to trace copyright owners, and the author and publisher apologize to anyone whose rights have inadvertently not been acknowledged. This will be corrected in any reprint.